# If There Are Horns

*poems by*

## francesca preston

*Finishing Line Press*
Georgetown, Kentucky

# If
# There
# Are
# Horns

## ACKNOWLEDGMENTS

These poems first appeared in the following journals and publications:

*Crab Creek Review*: "Calaveritas" and "Cavolo Nero"
*Walrus*: "Foothills"
*Stonecoast Review*: "Mazzafegati"
*Phoebe: A Journal of Literature and Art*: "Century Plant"
*Wild Words: Ferociously Nourishing Poetry*: "The Dream in the Garden"
*MALUS*: "Two Poets Fall"

Thank you to Sandra Anfang for early encouragement and feedback on this
manuscript; Brian Conery for the gorgeous cover design; Roberto Barison
for the photo of me in India; the Community of Writers summer workshops,
where several of these poems were written; Onie Kriegler for steady support;
and last but not leastly, to Cyrus Lark and Douglas Lerch for being in my life.

Publisher: Leah Huete de Maines
Editor: Christen Kincaid
Cover Art: Francesca Preston
Cover Design: Brian Conery
Author Photo: Roberto Barison

Order online: www.finishinglinepress.com
also available on amazon.com

Author inquiries and mail orders:
Finishing Line Press
PO Box 1626
Georgetown, Kentucky 40324
USA

# Table of Contents

*Dedicated to the ancestors, yours and mine*

"...Especially not a culture that dreams of eating without being eaten, and that offers the gods not even the guts or the crumbs."

Robert Bringhurst, *The Tree of Meaning*

# CALAVERITAS

From the bony ruts
of the fandango halls
frogs open
their trunks full of linen

Cold is still seated
on the hills
my ears
are opaque rooms

In the notes
of what went where
hurry has pulled
my letters tight

And this could be
the night Columbo switched
all the babies
while the women danced

The house sleeps
& realizes
its older
order

I came out
to feel the moon
little soft treat in
waxed paper

# FOOTHILLS

Because you've sought pardon from the road,
that its slick instructions stir you

The local yams & navel oranges

These straw-
berries and the word *Fresh*.

Because you have stuck with
the one arrow, slim bird fallen
from the horizon's clean
handshake

and that is has been ages now, you've
forgotten why you left, rising up only
to admire the fresco kiwis
ruined by rain.

Because you can always tighten yourself
to the highway's wind,
observe the tepid fields although
it's dark

Because you've been relying
on the skeleton ever since
the water left you

and why you are still bad
with your hands.

# CAVOLO NERO

Your mother dressed you
blind, cut your bangs all
the way to the roof.
Like Kore you have
mud on your wrists,
grab the nearest tree
when you hear him.
Still, no one sees you
fall languid past
neatly folded
cowshit, daffodil
stalks like the handles
of spoons.

Down here you wear
scarves, no sign of
your vast scarred
forehead. He feeds you
Cavolo Nero, that
calligraphic kale—
makes you pick it first,
black hair with neat
part. You break dirt, then
a hole without sleeves.
When your mother gets
you back she says why
do men always like
dark wood

# MAZZAFEGATI

Some have horses
in them, some
cattle: some
are eaten with
red pancakes,
or sweetly burned
apples, a dish called
*The Dead
Grandmother.*
The ones my mother
loves are probably
dark, no moons
of fat in them,
and curved slightly
like something
I won't say.
Blood bubbles,
salted baby arms,
kin.

# LIBERTY

The big silver dollars
smelled like old cheese
and even though I didn't like that
I always asked for the jar
up on the high kitchen shelf
with the passed-on plates.
I remember the bald men
with their profiles which
I pressed against my cheek.
Occasionally a woman
with contained hair.
I wanted to study them.
I wanted to eat them.
The coins were always there.
On the backs were the wings
of birds trapped in hot metal.
But now cool to my touch.
Sometimes a bell, unswinging.
I wanted it all. Their dates,
their words, their helmets,
their birds. How could I know
they'd own me as much?

# RUBBER BANDS

There are ten of you.
Leaning slightly
on each other
like cranky cells
too big for a microscope.
Three blue, one
the red of a dull tomato
and the rest of the band
is a color we know
well: tan noodle,
dun deal, *snap*.
Why throw you
away? You've got
so much promise,
heartbeats quickening
around newspapers,
mouths for mail.
You will even stretch
yourselves, like vipers,
for the largest things
I have: encyclopedias,
melons. But small
and shriveled my
Nana used to keep you
huddled up for warmth
on the doorknob,
where you would
kiss our paws
discreetly, and we
never said
anything.

# DRY YEARS

You offer me the sweet box of your room
and I say No. That I'm a twiner, roof
top inclined, that I want to watch the sun
roll out like a lavender cabbage.

I admire you epiphytically which
is to say I use you to get closer to
the light. *Hook, suck, coil*—even the blue
tattoo on your back like a well in ragged,

barren country. Cataclysmic thirst,
you can't say it enough, I think you've had
some lean, dry years and I imagine if
your boots were removed there would be feet

so fragile a mother might carry you home
and plant them in the knowing ground, unknowing.

# LYCHEES IN HEAVY SYRUP

1.
I can already feel your hand
on my foot, I bought the fruit
because I liked the can

We talk about gimmicks, decide
we've changed our mind
about art—

to name our dogs & children
with the same book

to love the hot angel
who skates in the microwave.

She is determined as we
would like to be.


2.

The full moon looks so eminently
normal, trounced by trees & gargling
its own clear blood

We're edging towards the ravine
of midnight, where only those
that can elaborate survive

You say you have not seen
the stars in such a long time,

And it becomes clear that
every road is the profile of a face.

3.

Epiphany, little black-
eyed bird:

*terror is a house*
*with no pen*

never vice versa

The body constructed
of long lines, moon a lychee
in heavy syrup

Your face is perfect & lovely
because of the way
the holes are arranged

and I will picture you

even when your skull
is a dried-out comb
and all the bees have left.

# RAW SISTER

I.
My sister the photographer has a crazy
hankering for the perfect
black fabric, deep as a dilated eye.

She says it must covet
all light and hide it, when shot
and developed give no indication of itself.

For now a faux-velvet skirt suffices,
torn by the one seam and hung plush-side up.
Cheerfully vain, her favorite subject is her own

deeply pale body: the nude wearing the one
black sock pulled knee-high is she, raw sister.
I think *amputee,* or *one-legged abalone*—

A traumatic disaster there, with the backdrop
so silent. The line between black cloth and sock
is missing, which frightens me and pleases her.

II.
My sister is growing less nuanced;
her goal, she says, is to be all one color.
Already, skin and hair are rushing

towards an odd middle ground—opal nacre,
roughed-up white. Her lipstick, too,
the same hue of a hangover.

Now her eyes are the only exception,
painted and painted and painted
until the lashes are blackened weeds.

To encounter her thus, naked, is to feel
(as I did) that you've received a sheet
of fine, ivory paper in the mail

Nearly blank, just one small word
typed fiercely upon it. You cannot
for the life of you avoid that one word.

# AEROGRAMME HOME

Here the morning says *no you can't have me*
unless you give yourself over, dirty
hibiscus & goat with an udder

like an upturned mosque—become these
things, vanish. The sign on the gate of
the tall white house has the silhouette

of a howling animal, it says "Be Aware
of Dog." So beautiful I can't believe it.
People walk. People gesture. Boys in ivory

knee socks stand on their toes to mail
a letter. Men drink tea from tiny
cups. The smell of shit, then gone.

Here you watch the same scene
as the children who squat on the very edge
of the road, leaving small brown knots

underneath them. They seem wonderfully calm,
they talk to their friends across the way.
Everything is fine.

In fact everything is perfect, even if
we are not happy about it. A woman
bends over me, says Wow! That's clever!

To write a letter! and we laugh.
Soon I will finish, open a newspaper
to read about war & its odd numbers.

It will be much the same as yesterday,
someone will be saying *disintegrate*
or *surrender*

# CENTURY PLANT

Stenciled word of your
body I
forgot to love broke

Thirteen doll heads on
the mantle
family of bad fruit

Bottom of the hold
needles in
yarn, wrasse at coral

Charred wood & last night
skeins of black
hair in the burn pile

New names for muscles
the agave
cactus blooms just once

Nightgown, numbered limbs
the house was
moved here by donkey

Face full of windmills
now we pay
the turbulence gods

# RENTAL

Driven by lack or
leisure, what strikes
the lavender
bicycle as odd
is freedom: no lock
in this girl's hands, no
expectation he'll
be waiting, even.

She seems to
know what it's like
being silent in a country
where the backs of trucks say
*Use Horn OK Please.*
The two of them swerve.
Life has made them mute
and uninhibited.

Not to say that she is
perfect. Dawdles &
the kickstand irks her,
doesn't hold weight.
Today she leans him
(softly) up against
the Maharajah's
Cadillac, goes in.

# ORCHID

The father so strong
you used to put

three layers of white
underwear on before

bed is showing me
how to milk a goat.

The milk and pail
make a tiny sound,

unmappable as an
orchid and slow going

too—the milk is a cyclone
and I am at the center

of it, squeezing and
cinching until the goat's

legs quiver and when
the milk finally comes

we all laugh w/ relief.

# THE DREAM IN THE GARDEN

if music is the sound of fingertips
hitting a jug
in which someone once
carried water

mother
what purpose
in my growing beyond
your dream of my birth?

many times i've watched you
have it, the dream in the garden
where i emerge:

an old wooden clothespin
with cornsilk hair

you clip me to your breast then,
as if to jumpstart it

and after     throw me away
for a reason i have not yet figured out

mother i was born with a body
thickly settled, dense
as a pomegranate

not a fruit steeped in the syrup
it will taste of

i was already hard
with the things
i had selected for myself

inside you i was
choosing and discarding
without lifting
a finger, i was

like the girl
in the department
store, deciding what
to steal

# TWO POETS FALL

They both know that poems
are maps of dead rivers

that a word is a tree
burnt out by lightning
but still living

She whispers

       *boneyard apples*

and he stumbles down and through
the hot, hollow grass
as if after an animal named
and lost in the same instant.

Yes: we lived and died
before we wrote.

# CORPSE FLOWER

You opened the day
we promised you wouldn't.
For six months nothing.
Single, lanky leaf.
We had no reason
to expect your room
sized bloom, the red door
frame of your petal's
edges. By the time
we came you'd put
the rot out, like a cat
into the night, and shut.
Now we sniff your stoop
and wait for children,
your bright, acidic fruit.

## GO ADORNED IN CHAINS
## OF SAUSAGES


If an animal present himself to you
grab a knife quick and lick
the blade for good luck. Make night,
bring the bucket. The wound
is a place between worlds.

Empty now the inside sawn:
Keep the parts whole and dry.
If a tongue wristles against
you relax. No one
is watching.

One container may seem
small. Soften the hard lines
of tendon, grind the rest.

If there are horns
give them to a young girl.

Boil the fluids ilky to your own.
*Bita. Blot. Volumen.*
Write until there's nothing left
but skin and bone.

# LUGANEGA

Curvy, your small
violin plays
by the meter,
drawing out the smell
of shit mixed with
blood. If I could be
anywhere all at once
it would be here,
where the strong-breasted
women salt meat.
Pine nuts are all the
jewels we have, &
they shine in the pot of
flesh while it cooks,
*while it cooks,*
*while it cooks.*

# NOTES

Calaveritas is a ghost town in the Sierra foothills of Calaveras Country, California.

Kore is another name for Persephone, the Greek goddess. Abducted by Hades, she becomes the queen of the underworld, and her return each year to mother Demeter, goddess of agriculture, signifies Spring.

The gigantic corpse flower, *Titan arum*, is notorious for its brief bloom that smells of rotting flesh. The UC Berkeley Botanical Garden is home to the Titan arum, which occasionally disappoints its fans by blooming overnight when no one is there.

Luganega and Mazzafegati are both names of traditional Italian sausages.

*"Go adorned in Chains of Sausages"* is from letterist and lexicographer James Howell (1600s). The rest of the sentence reads "Mutton, beef, and bacon are to her as the Will, Understanding, and Memory are to the Soul; Cabbages, Turnips, Artichokes, Potatoes, and Dates are her five Senses, and Pepper the Common-sense; she must have Marrow to keep Life in her, and some Birds to make her light; by all means she must go adorned with Chains of Sausages."

Francesca Preston is a writer, editor, and visual artist based in Petaluma, California. She is a graduate of Amherst College, a two-time grad school dropout, and an ongoing student of herbalism, etymology, and place-based art practices. A version of her chapbook *This Was Like I Said All Gone*, devoted to voices from the ghost town of her ancestors, is available from Ghost City Press. Francesca graduated *summa cum laude* from Amherst, where she won prizes for her thesis "Still Uncodified," on the compositional process of American poet Amy Clampitt. Her family has operated Preston Farm & Winery in Sonoma County for nearly fifty years. francescapreston.com

www.ingramcontent.com/pod-product-compliance
Lightning Source LLC
LaVergne TN
LVHW041329080426
835513LV00008B/656